The White Stripes

First published in Great Britain in 2005
by Artnik
341b Queenstown Road
London SW8 4LH
UK

ISBN 1–903906-97-0

Design: Supriya Sahai
Research: Rav Karyal
Pictures: Live Photography
Book Concept: Nicholas Artsrunik
Editor: John McVicar

Printed and bound in Spain by Gráficas Díaz

The
White & Stripes

To Stevie, Steve, Simon & Mr Chang – keepers of the flame.

Acknowledgements

I like The White Stripes. A lot. And I've had the pleasure of meeting Jack and Meg on a number of occasions. This book doesn't profess to be the definitive biography – it is an unofficial tribute to their career so far, by someone who respects what they're doing. In a relatively short space of time they've added something of great value to the musical climate, and that's no mean feat.

To chart their career so far I have drawn on news stories, interviews and features that have appeared in the following publications. I'm particularly grateful to the **Evening Standard** which had the foresight to let me commission - what I believe was - the first White Stripes interview to ever appear in a UK newspaper or magazine. This book wouldn't have been possible without the recollections and writings of Stevie Chick. Thanks also to the staff at the British Library and to Rav for all her help as research assistant.

Alex Hannaford

Evening Standard
Los Angeles Times
Guardian
Daily Mail
Mail on Sunday
Independent
Independent on Sunday
Daily Mirror
Sunday Mirror
The Scotsman
Express
Spin Magazine
Time Magazine
Daily Telegraph
Washington Post
Chicago Tribune
NME
Kerrang!
Sunday People
Mojo magazine
The New Yorker
Boston Globe
Rolling Stone
The Sun
Manchester Evening News
The Times

Glasgow Herald & Sunday Herald
Birmingham Evening Mail
The Scotsman
Daily Record
Observer
Coventry Evening Telegraph
Sunday Times

bbc.co.uk
www.whitestripes.com
www.tripletremelo.com
www.whitestripes.net
www.redcandycane.net
www.geocities.com/brainborder/
whitestripes/whitestripes.html

ITE STRIPES

LWIND HEAT

DOORS7 SHOW

Detroit... An empty, desolate – but at the same time hauntingly beautiful – city on the banks of Lake Michigan. Downtown you can't walk out alone at night for fear of being mugged. People drive round with their car doors locked and walkways take office workers from one tall, glass-fronted building to another.

It's not safe but it's far from soulless.

While its residents still suffered the legacy of race riots from the late 1960s, Motown and the rock 'n' roll explosion of the Stooges, Iggy Pop and the MC5, became a unifying force.

A violent history couldn't stifle the city's creativity and burning desire for change. While crack addicts, their lips blue and their faces buried in paper bags of glue, walked the streets or sat, hunched in doorways, back in the late 1990s, behind the walls of its handful of venues, something very special was stirring.

Welcome to GREAT LAKES GR

Ten minutes drive from downtown, Sixties-infused rock 'n' roll poured from local club The Magic Stick, while the crowd inside, downing bottles of local Ghettoblaster beer and cheap whisky shots, coolly tapped their feet to the band onstage.

The garage rock scene was erupting, still exciting, subversive, and still relatively hard to find. It had become *the new soundtrack for a disaffected generation.*

At the back of the venue, twentysomethings decked out in thrift-store Levis, band T-shirts (the obscurer the better) and Detroit-original black Brookes leather jackets, crowded around the bar.

Three bands were on the bill that cold April night – Ko and the Knockouts, The Come Ons and the Von Bondies – all part of the revolutionary new wave of made-in-Michigan rock 'n' roll. It was a powerful force, set against the backdrop of a deserted but beautiful city, peppered with incredible derelict suburban mansions, turn-of-the-century houses and empty downtown office blocks.

Here, the city's kids were rocking to the new sound, spearheaded by the leading lights of the scene – The White Stripes.

KO and the knockouts

Von Bondies

Michigan

Welcome to Detroit

The Renaissance Ci

Founded 1701

THE Come Ons

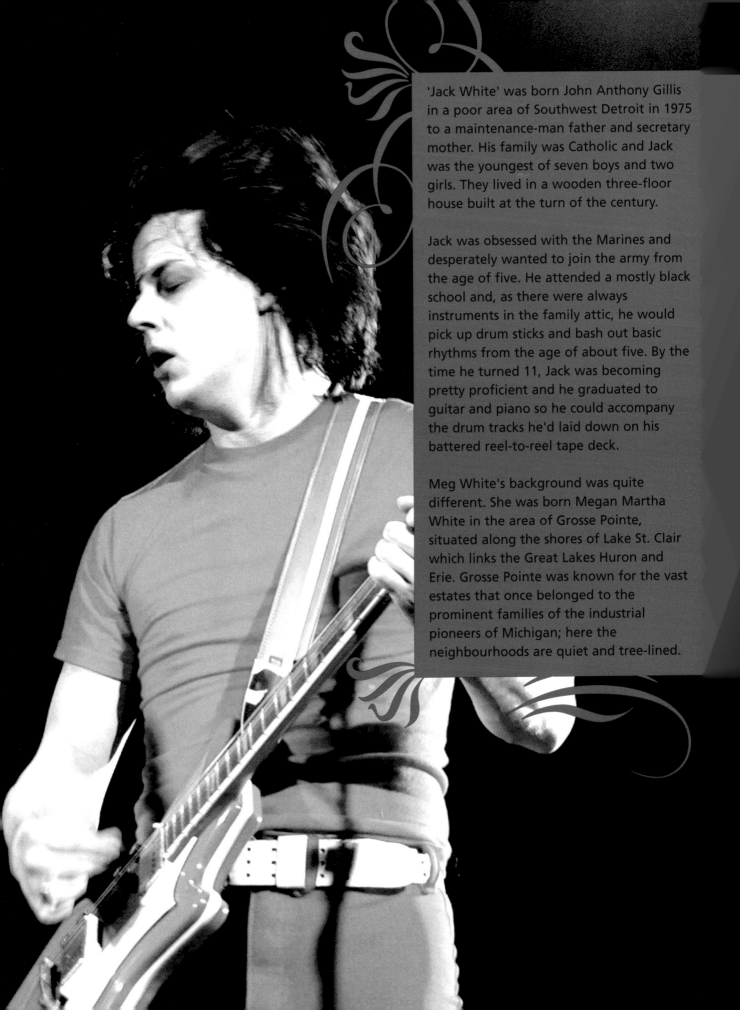

'Jack White' was born John Anthony Gillis in a poor area of Southwest Detroit in 1975 to a maintenance-man father and secretary mother. His family was Catholic and Jack was the youngest of seven boys and two girls. They lived in a wooden three-floor house built at the turn of the century.

Jack was obsessed with the Marines and desperately wanted to join the army from the age of five. He attended a mostly black school and, as there were always instruments in the family attic, he would pick up drum sticks and bash out basic rhythms from the age of about five. By the time he turned 11, Jack was becoming pretty proficient and he graduated to guitar and piano so he could accompany the drum tracks he'd laid down on his battered reel-to-reel tape deck.

Meg White's background was quite different. She was born Megan Martha White in the area of Grosse Pointe, situated along the shores of Lake St. Clair which links the Great Lakes Huron and Erie. Grosse Pointe was known for the vast estates that once belonged to the prominent families of the industrial pioneers of Michigan; here the neighbourhoods are quiet and tree-lined.

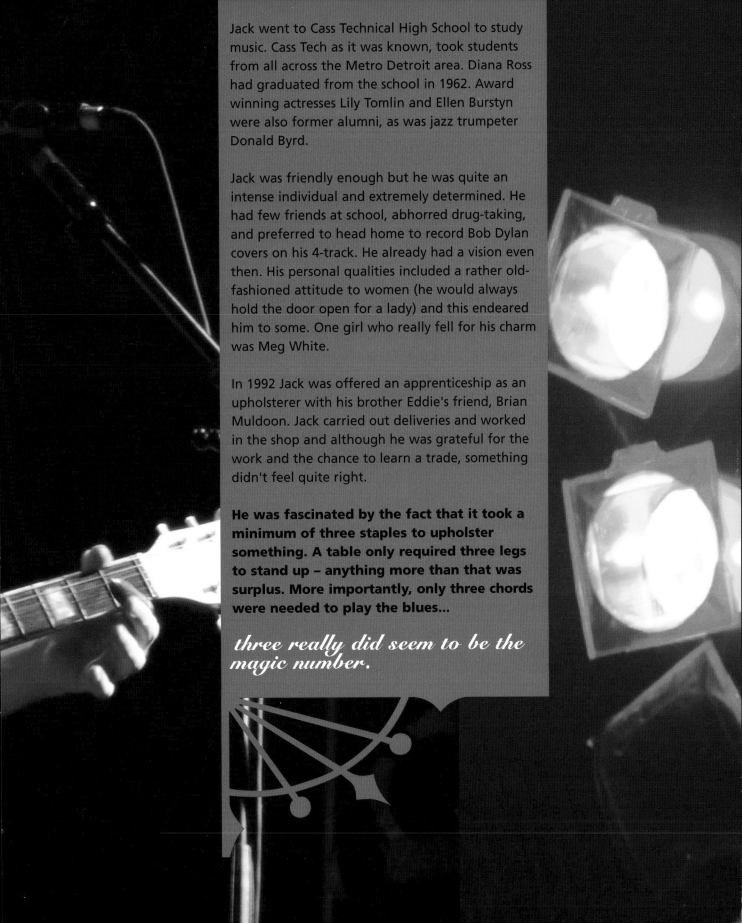

Jack went to Cass Technical High School to study music. Cass Tech as it was known, took students from all across the Metro Detroit area. Diana Ross had graduated from the school in 1962. Award winning actresses Lily Tomlin and Ellen Burstyn were also former alumni, as was jazz trumpeter Donald Byrd.

Jack was friendly enough but he was quite an intense individual and extremely determined. He had few friends at school, abhorred drug-taking, and preferred to head home to record Bob Dylan covers on his 4-track. He already had a vision even then. His personal qualities included a rather old-fashioned attitude to women (he would always hold the door open for a lady) and this endeared him to some. One girl who really fell for his charm was Meg White.

In 1992 Jack was offered an apprenticeship as an upholsterer with his brother Eddie's friend, Brian Muldoon. Jack carried out deliveries and worked in the shop and although he was grateful for the work and the chance to learn a trade, something didn't feel quite right.

He was fascinated by the fact that it took a minimum of three staples to upholster something. A table only required three legs to stand up – anything more than that was surplus. More importantly, only three chords were needed to play the blues...

three really did seem to be the magic number.

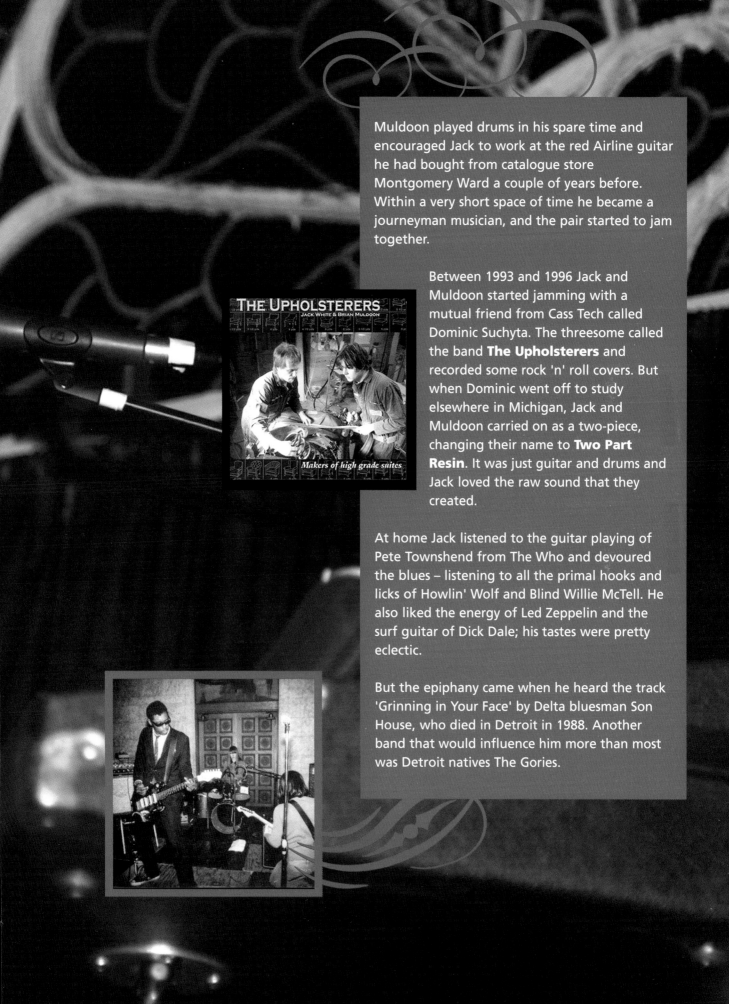

Muldoon played drums in his spare time and encouraged Jack to work at the red Airline guitar he had bought from catalogue store Montgomery Ward a couple of years before. Within a very short space of time he became a journeyman musician, and the pair started to jam together.

Between 1993 and 1996 Jack and Muldoon started jamming with a mutual friend from Cass Tech called Dominic Suchyta. The threesome called the band **The Upholsterers** and recorded some rock 'n' roll covers. But when Dominic went off to study elsewhere in Michigan, Jack and Muldoon carried on as a two-piece, changing their name to **Two Part Resin**. It was just guitar and drums and Jack loved the raw sound that they created.

At home Jack listened to the guitar playing of Pete Townshend from The Who and devoured the blues – listening to all the primal hooks and licks of Howlin' Wolf and Blind Willie McTell. He also liked the energy of Led Zeppelin and the surf guitar of Dick Dale; his tastes were pretty eclectic.

But the epiphany came when he heard the track 'Grinning in Your Face' by Delta bluesman Son House, who died in Detroit in 1988. Another band that would influence him more than most was Detroit natives The Gories.

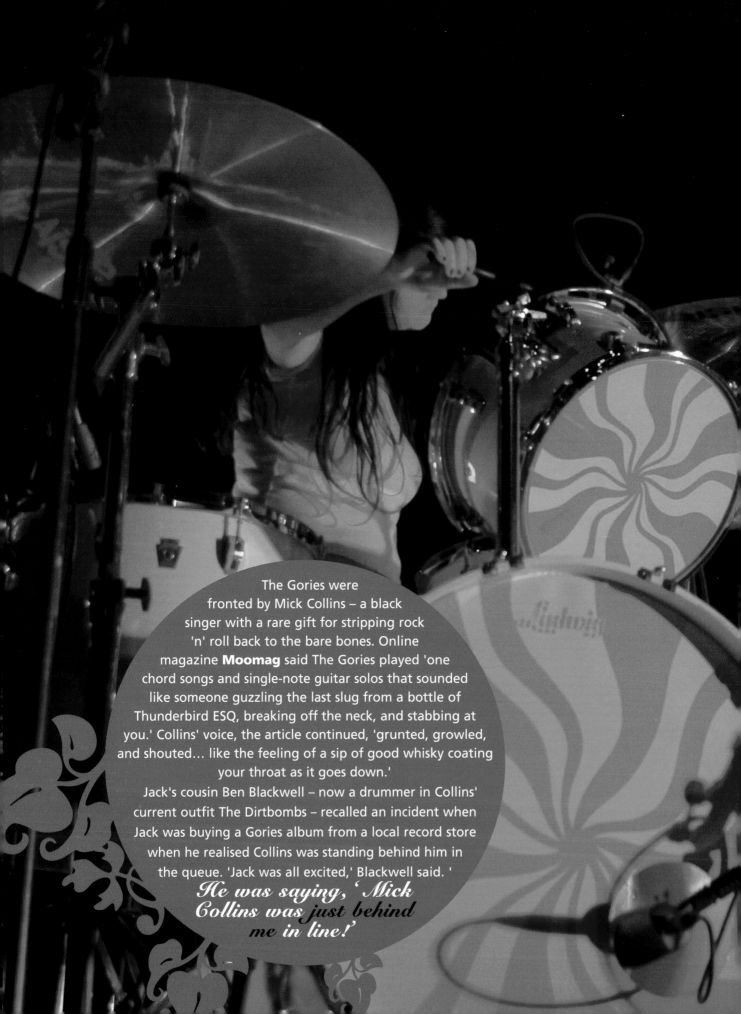

The Gories were fronted by Mick Collins – a black singer with a rare gift for stripping rock 'n' roll back to the bare bones. Online magazine **Moomag** said The Gories played 'one chord songs and single-note guitar solos that sounded like someone guzzling the last slug from a bottle of Thunderbird ESQ, breaking off the neck, and stabbing at you.' Collins' voice, the article continued, 'grunted, growled, and shouted… like the feeling of a sip of good whisky coating your throat as it goes down.'

Jack's cousin Ben Blackwell – now a drummer in Collins' current outfit The Dirtbombs – recalled an incident when Jack was buying a Gories album from a local record store when he realised Collins was standing behind him in the queue. 'Jack was all excited,' Blackwell said. '*He was saying, 'Mick Collins was just behind me in line!'*

By 1994 Jack had also joined local country punk act Goober and the Peas as a drummer, appearing on their records as 'Jack Gillis'.

His parents had moved to a different area of Detroit and Jack had stayed on in the family home, letting various friends rent out the other rooms. He had a drum kit set up on the top floor but decided to teach himself to play the upright piano his parents had left behind.

He painted the inside of the house red and white – everything, from the walls to the kitchen units; even his record player had a red and white turntable. And he also indulged his fascination with stuffed animals.

The heads of deer, moose and elk jutted out from the walls in his living room.

It looked like a cross between a 1960s vintage furniture shop in Camden market and a hunting ranch.

In 1996 Jack and Meg married at a farm in South Lyon, southwestern Oakland County, in front of a small gathering of family and friends. Jack took Meg's surname. At the time Meg was working in a blues bar called Memphis Smoke in the smart Detroit suburb of Royal Oak while Jack, who had by now quit working for Muldoon, struggled to get his own upholstery business off the ground – Third Man Upholstery.

Meanwhile Muldoon went on to form a band with Jack's brother Eddie called Tin Knocker. Sometime after their wedding, Meg was messing about on the top floor of their house and began to thump out a beat on Jack's drum-kit. Jack started to accompany his wife on guitar, playing a David Bowie number. She'd only ever played violin as a small child before, and though she was far from perfect on the drums, Jack loved her primal, almost childlike attempt. It was raw and basic, but it worked.

The White Stripes was born –
the name of the band taken
from the striped peppermint
candy that Meg loved.

And in this two-piece, unlike any other band Jack had been in before, he found he could change key mid-song. Musically, he gelled with Meg in a way he hadn't with anyone else. It was instinctive, atavistic, primeval.

The White Stripes played their first show in August 1997, opening for The Hentchmen at Detroit's Gold Dollar – another great garage rock venue along with the Magic Stick and Lagerhouse.

The Hentchmen featured John Szymanski on organ, harmonica and vocals, 'Tim V. Eight' on guitar, and Mike Latulippe on drums. Their '60s-influenced garage rock had seen them become one of the prominent Detroit bands in a career that spanned 10 years and they had signed to New York's Norton Records back in 1992. Meg had only been playing drums two months, edgy but whisky steadied the nerves.

At first it was quite hard to be taken seriously. When nearly every rock 'n' roll band in Detroit was a five-piece, climbing on stage with just a drum kit and guitarist was tantamount to musical suicide.

But everyone there that first night went home remembering the songs; those stripped-down blues songs that just stuck in the mind.

From their very first gig, The White Stripes were indelible.

Towards the end of the year Dave Buick, a friend of Jack's who ran a small indie label called Italy Records, offered to put out the first White Stripes single. Buick had already released seven inches from Rocket 455 – a high-energy street rock band that was spearheading the Detroit underground rock scene – and would later issue records by The Hentchmen, Soledad Brothers, Clone Defects and Whirlwind Heat.

The first White Stripes 7" was a clear, red vinyl version of their song 'Let's Shake Hands'. Buick pressed 500 copies in 1997.

Later, in 2002 when the band had hit the big time he re-pressed the record, releasing 2000 copies of the second edition on limited edition black vinyl.

After 'Let's Shake Hands', Buick released 'Lafayette Blues' which Jack would later introduce on stage as 'his only French song'. Jack was still dividing his time between bands and had joined R&B outfit The Go as a second guitarist. Stick-thin singer Bobby Harlow's stage presence was mesmerising but Jack added his unmistakeable high-pitched screaming vocal and guitar licks to the mix. The Go became the biggest band on the Detroit garage scene, and soon Seattle's legendary Sub Pop Records – once home to Nirvana – came knocking at the door.

If Jack had signed the deal, Sub Pop would have had automatic rights to all the White Stripes material as well. Logic told him not to sign. He appeared on the Go's debut record and then quit the band to concentrate on the two-piece he'd started with Meg.

Jack and Meg's friends The Detroit Cobras – a garage rock four-piece that played mostly covers, including raw, throaty versions of songs by the Marvalettes and Otis Redding – were signed to the indie label Sympathy for the Record Industry, better known as simply Sympathy Records. The company was run by the elusive and evocatively-titled Long Gone John from an office in Long Beach, California. John had famously released one record a week for the past 13 years and boasted of having been home to over 500 bands during that time. One of these was the Detroit Cobras.

The Cobras' then-guitarist Steve Shaw told John he should check out the White Stripes.

And after listening to the two 7" releases on Italy Records he was sold. **He signed them without ever seeing Jack and Meg live.**

The White Stripes set to work recording their debut album at local studio Ghetto Recorders, run by the Dirtbombs guitarist Jim Diamond. Diamond was a larger-than-life no-nonsense muso with a dry sense of humour. Using vintage equipment at the studio built in the back of his sprawling downtown home, Diamond also knew how to make an album sound great.

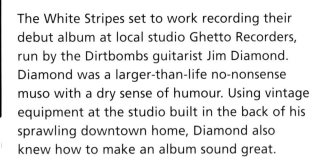

'We were going for a stinky kind of sound,' he recalled.

The White Stripes eponymous debut included cover versions of Robert Johnson's 'Stop Breaking Down Blues' and Bob Dylan's 'One More Cup Of Coffee' as well as original numbers 'When I Hear My Name' and the pained 'Wasting My Time'.

But no one dared accuse Jack White of 'ripping off' the blues. 'I'm not interested in copying – at all,' he would later say. 'I'm interested in re-telling the story. Music has been storytelling and melody for thousands of years, and it's not going to change. And certainly I am not going to try to change it.'

Playing stripped-down, back-to-basics rhythm and blues required back-to-basics instruments, and you couldn't get more basic than Jack's precious Airline guitar – which in the 1960s was one of the cheapest on the market.

Add to that Meg's basic drum set-up, an occasional Fender Rhodes piano and '60s Kay acoustic guitar,

and The White Stripes were in their element.

The songs 'Astro' with its raucous energy, and the fast-paced, primal 'Jimmy the Exloder' – a story Jack had made up about a monkey who exploded things that weren't painted red – hinted at the direction the White Stripes would be heading in future.

The album cost less than £1,000 to make.

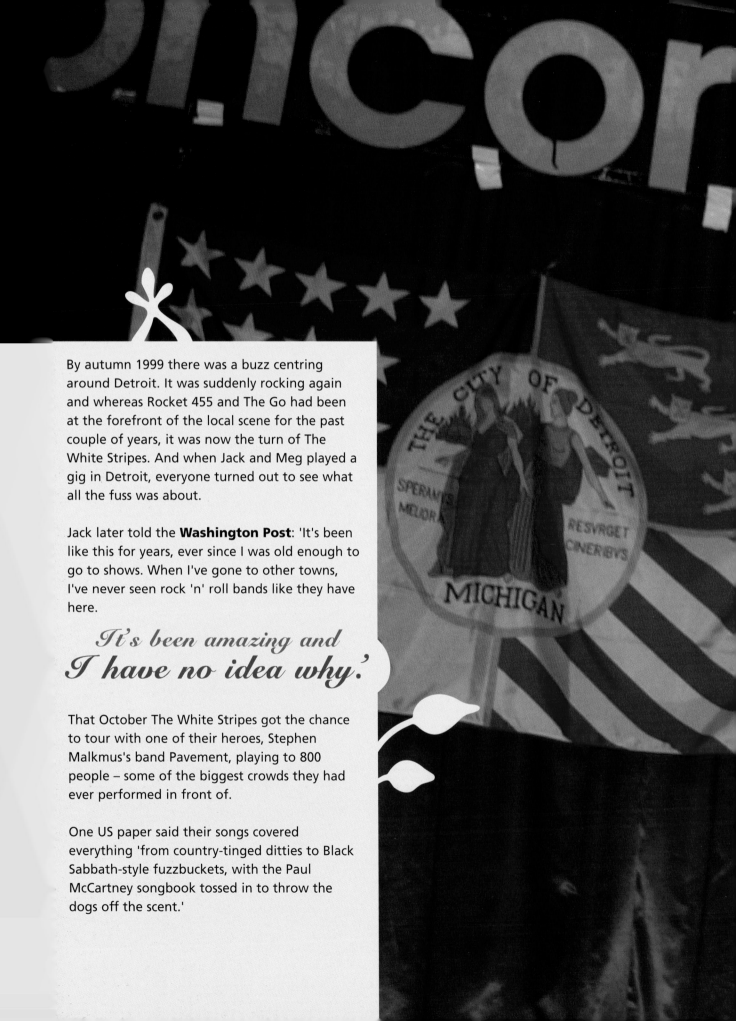

By autumn 1999 there was a buzz centring around Detroit. It was suddenly rocking again and whereas Rocket 455 and The Go had been at the forefront of the local scene for the past couple of years, it was now the turn of The White Stripes. And when Jack and Meg played a gig in Detroit, everyone turned out to see what all the fuss was about.

Jack later told the **Washington Post**: 'It's been like this for years, ever since I was old enough to go to shows. When I've gone to other towns, I've never seen rock 'n' roll bands like they have here.

It's been amazing and
I have no idea why.'

That October The White Stripes got the chance to tour with one of their heroes, Stephen Malkmus's band Pavement, playing to 800 people – some of the biggest crowds they had ever performed in front of.

One US paper said their songs covered everything 'from country-tinged ditties to Black Sabbath-style fuzzbuckets, with the Paul McCartney songbook tossed in to throw the dogs off the scent.'

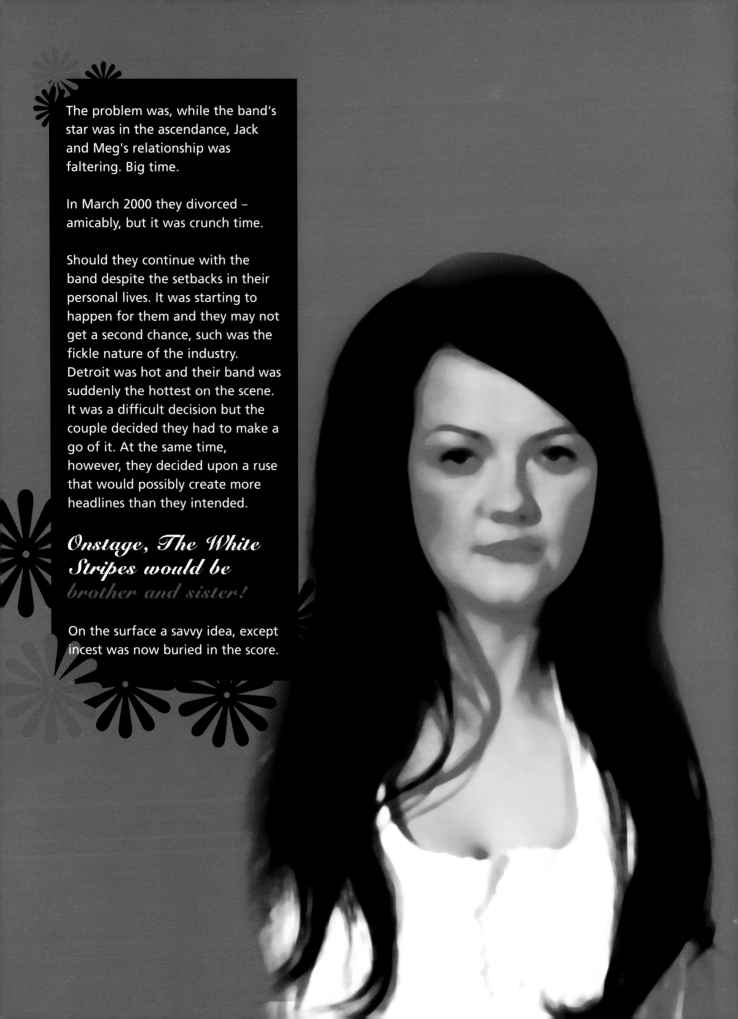

The problem was, while the band's star was in the ascendance, Jack and Meg's relationship was faltering. Big time.

In March 2000 they divorced – amicably, but it was crunch time.

Should they continue with the band despite the setbacks in their personal lives. It was starting to happen for them and they may not get a second chance, such was the fickle nature of the industry. Detroit was hot and their band was suddenly the hottest on the scene. It was a difficult decision but the couple decided they had to make a go of it. At the same time, however, they decided upon a ruse that would possibly create more headlines than they intended.

Onstage, The White Stripes would be *brother and sister!*

On the surface a savvy idea, except incest was now buried in the score.

While it might attract possibly unwanted media attention, it would be benign attention, not the intrusive, below the belt stuff of journos always on the prowl for the sex angle. They certainly didn't want to discuss their personal life – especially as it was still so sensitive.

So Jack and Meg would be the youngest two siblings in a family of 10 children. And even if that wasn't the truth, in reality, as far as The White Stripes were concerned, it was all part of the act.

It was a kind of rock 'n' roll truth.

The problem was success was always going to expose the real truth.

Then came *De Stijl*

The White Stripes' second album, recorded on an 8-track in Jack's living room, was named after the Dutch abstract art movement – literally translated 'the style'. Long Gone John later told one newspaper: 'It wasn't until I finally saw them around the time of De Stijl that I thought, Jesus Christ, what have I got here...'

Jack told **Maximum RocknRoll** magazine that, whereas their debut sounded angry, with *De Stijl* the duo had 'tried to get a little cleaner'. He said, Maybe we changed from anger to bitterness.'

The record contained the sing-a-long 'You're Pretty Good Looking (For a Girl)', Beatles-esque 'Apple Blossom', raw blues workout 'Death Letter', and the beautiful 'Truth Doesn't Make a Noise', with its evocative lyric: 'The motion of her tiny hands / and the quiver of her bones below / are the signs of a girl alone / and tell you everything you need to know.'

Rolling Stone magazine described *De Stijl* as 'feisty and clever, full of scuzzy garage rock that would fit nicely on a Nuggets compilation between the Sonics and the Standells'.

The band's local paper the **Detroit Metro Times** reported: 'The Whites are now decorating the rooms of their mansion with Dylan-worthy introspection and minimalism, primal howls and cathartic regression (oh, yeah, and the occasional "rock anthem").

Translation? It's fucking brilliant.'

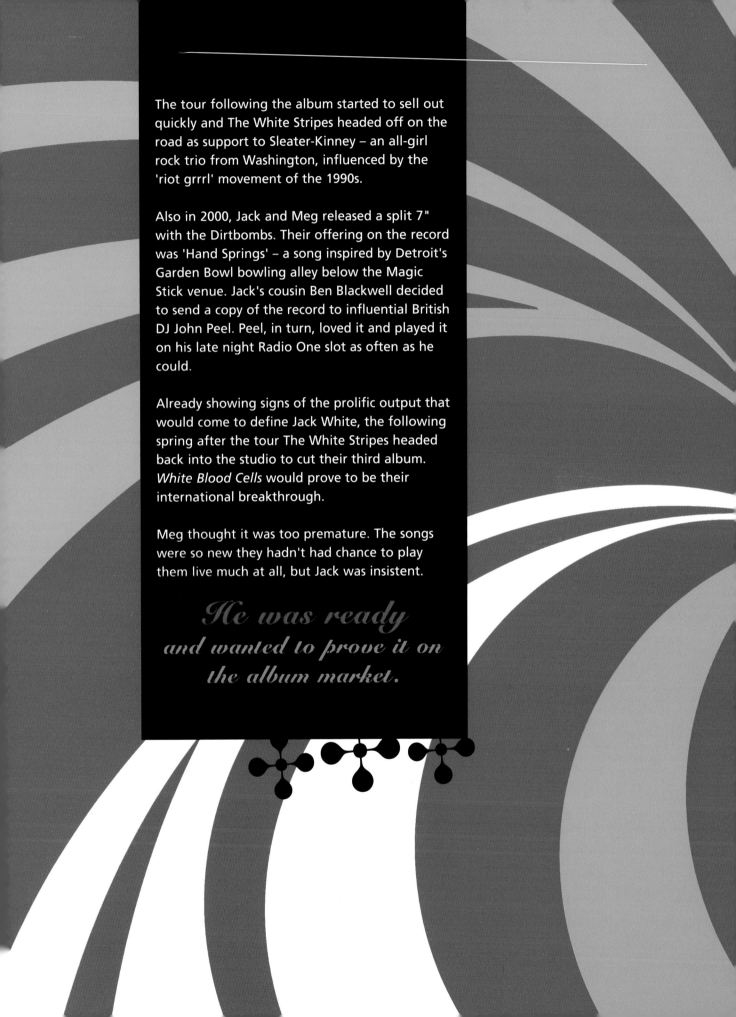

The tour following the album started to sell out quickly and The White Stripes headed off on the road as support to Sleater-Kinney – an all-girl rock trio from Washington, influenced by the 'riot grrrl' movement of the 1990s.

Also in 2000, Jack and Meg released a split 7" with the Dirtbombs. Their offering on the record was 'Hand Springs' – a song inspired by Detroit's Garden Bowl bowling alley below the Magic Stick venue. Jack's cousin Ben Blackwell decided to send a copy of the record to influential British DJ John Peel. Peel, in turn, loved it and played it on his late night Radio One slot as often as he could.

Already showing signs of the prolific output that would come to define Jack White, the following spring after the tour The White Stripes headed back into the studio to cut their third album. *White Blood Cells* would prove to be their international breakthrough.

Meg thought it was too premature. The songs were so new they hadn't had chance to play them live much at all, but Jack was insistent.

He was ready and wanted to prove it on the album market.

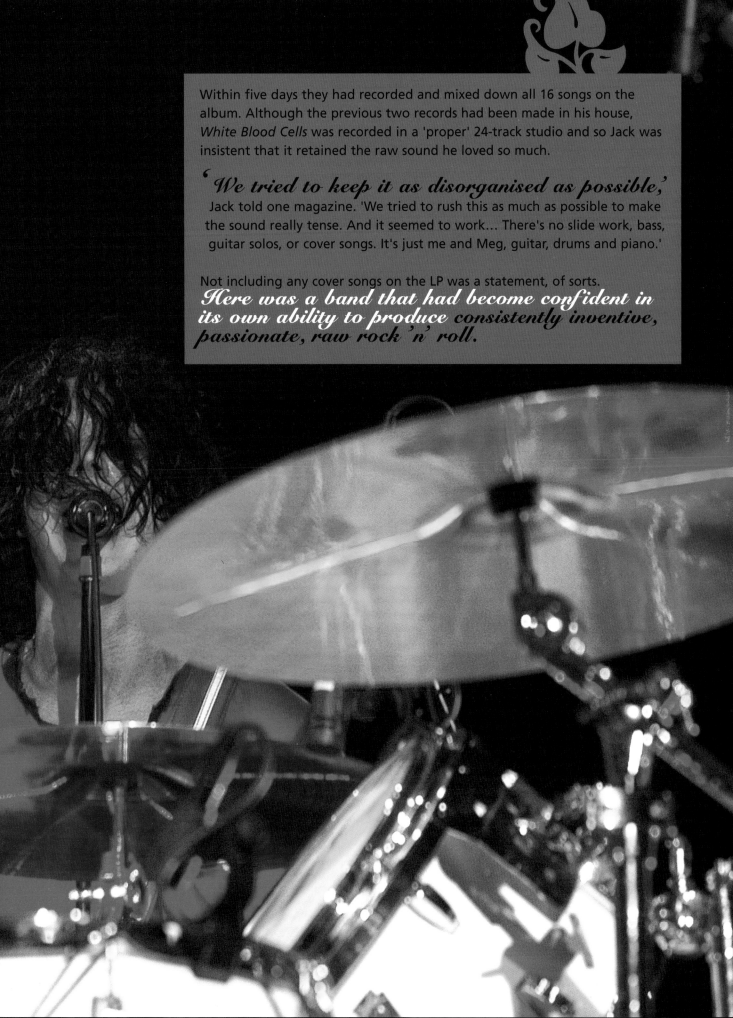

Within five days they had recorded and mixed down all 16 songs on the album. Although the previous two records had been made in his house, *White Blood Cells* was recorded in a 'proper' 24-track studio and so Jack was insistent that it retained the raw sound he loved so much.

'*We tried to keep it as disorganised as possible,*' Jack told one magazine. 'We tried to rush this as much as possible to make the sound really tense. And it seemed to work… There's no slide work, bass, guitar solos, or cover songs. It's just me and Meg, guitar, drums and piano.'

Not including any cover songs on the LP was a statement, of sorts. *Here was a band that had become confident in its own ability to produce consistently inventive, passionate, raw rock 'n' roll.*

With *White Blood Cells* they had stepped up a gear from *De Stijl*. It still went for the catchy hooks ('Hotel Yorba') and sing-a-long, sometimes childlike folk numbers ('We're Going to be Friends'), but songs like 'I'm Finding it Harder to be Gentleman' oozed bluesy introspection and 'Fell in Love with a Girl' was dirty, loud garage rock at its meatiest best.

The album was so diverse, so interesting, it was little wonder that it would become the key to their international success.

'Hotel Yorba' – the catchy first single that would trumpet their arrival in the UK – was a paean to a hotel a few blocks from Jack's house. It was a run-down hole, now populated by homeless bums, alcoholics and crack addicts but rumour had it that the Beatles once stayed there.

The rumour was completely untrue but it was a good story.

The cover art featured Jack and Meg against a red backdrop, apparently being attacked by a group of shadowy figures. But inside the album, the attackers were revealed to be the paparazzi – an allusion to the increasing media attention they were getting.

Before the release of *White Blood Cells* Jack told **Spin Magazine** 'at some point it would be nice if garage rock got a little bit of attention, because you get sick of playing in front of the same 50 people your whole life.

It would be nice for some bands to experience playing in front of 500 people.'

It was to be one of the most prophetic sentences he would utter. After their third album the White Stripes would get audiences... in spades.

When the album was released on Sympathy Records on June 26th, the **New York Times** announced that with *White Blood Cells* the band had achieved something uncanny. 'They have made rock rock again by returning to its origins as a simple, primitive sound full of unfettered zeal.'

The **Los Angeles Time**s described their LA gig as 'a rare display of humble showmanship as Jack bounced between two microphones singing and playing guitar, while Meg, pigtails swinging, beat on the drums with the enthusiasm of a child who'd learned them only yesterday.' Which was kind of true.

Then in March 2001, a writer for the **Detroit Free Press** wrote a story exposing Jack and Meg as divorcees. The paper published local county records that showed John Gillis had got hitched to Megan White in 1996 and that they had divorced four years later.

At a gig in Kalamazoo, Michigan – a city that was once a fur trading post back in the 1700s – Jack was unequivocal. 'Why can't people just write about the music?' he asked the audience. 'Why do they have to worry about our personal lives?' It was a hopelessly naive appeal but the audience didn't care.

As far as Jack and Meg were concerned, they got on well enough offstage and that was all that mattered.

'*The important part of a two-piece band is you* can't take sides,'

Jack later said. 'There's not a third person to take someone's side and call off the tension.'

Later that same month The White Stripes hit Austin, Texas.

Stevie Chick – at the time a hack for the **New Musical Express** – had walked the four miles or so from his tiny room at the Days Inn Motel on the edge of the six-lane i35 freeway, to Sixth Street – the main drag downtown which boasts more music venues, bars and tattoo parlours per square foot than downtown Detroit.

To get there, he had to go via the sprawling campus of the University of Texas – the biggest in the U.S. And as the sun started to drop in the sky, bathing the city of Austin in its warm red glow, Stevie took a couple of minutes to ponder what wonders were waiting for him that night.

This was no ordinary Wednesday evening at the end of March. This was the first night of the South by Southwest music festival - better known by its acronym SXSW – dubbed 'Spring Break for the music industry', and a place where the rock 'n' roll stars of the future were made.

And that night Stevie was in for a treat.

Since 1999 ~The White Stripes' records had only been available on import in the UK from Sympathy Records, via Cargo in London. The discs had been steadily moving off the shelves in independent record stores like Rough Trade, and Cargo's Simon Keeler had sent them to a handful of journalists he thought may like to review them. One of them was Stevie.

The cover of the CDs intrigued him – one featured a dark-haired, floppy-fringed boy and an enchanting-looking girl with jet-black hair and pale skin. Both were wearing white clothing and they were standing a couple of feet apart, surrounded by oblong blocks of red and white against a black backdrop. It was striking. The other record was slightly simpler: the same floppy-fringed boy, this time wearing white T-shirt and red trousers, and the girl was wearing a red body stocking. Both stood against a red backdrop with a little peppermint candy between their feet. When Stevie first played those LPs he was blown away. 'It is rock'n'roll born again,' he wrote in the NME. 'Stripped back to its barest elements, dipped in dirt and sex and explosive passion, and sent reeling into the future... to save rock 'n' roll, The White Stripes went back to the roots.' Even before he set foot on Texan soil, he had clearly already converted. But he still had to see them live.

And that's when the magic
really happened.

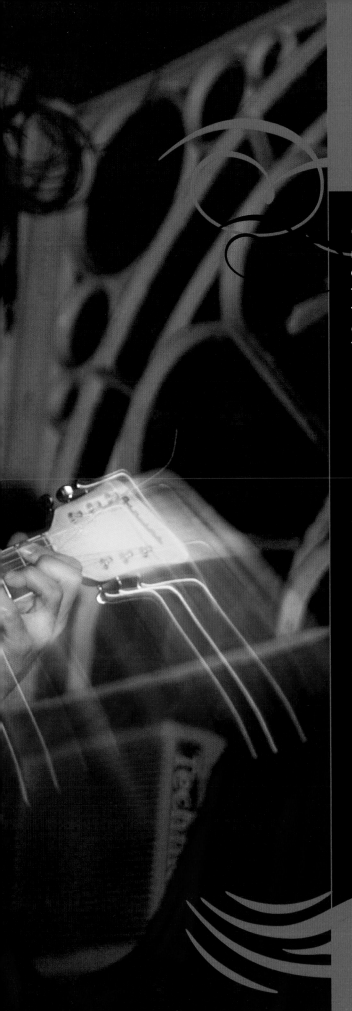

'It was my turn in the tattooist's chair,' Stevie recalls, 'and a fair amount of natural cowardice crept up my spine. As I stood in the doorway of the parlour, thinking of excuses not to go through with it, I gazed out upon Red River, calmly sizzling in the high afternoon sun. Then I heard **it**. 'It' being...

a lizard-lazy slick of slide guitar, a strangled yelp, and slow, heavy drums beating out a tattoo like a tank piling through a crumbling brick wall.

The sound of that weird, obscure Detroit band whose album, *De Stijl*, I'd been obsessing about since January.'

Stevie had to think on his feet. Grabbing his photographer Steve Gullick, who was sporting a fresh 'X' tattooed on his forearm, he ran across to Fat Tuesday's – the venue from where the noise was pouring.

'We snuck close to the stage,' Stevie remembers. 'It was the afternoon, so the venues were open to all-comers, not just the music industry bods – all getting more and more electrified by the magnetic figure onstage, sweating and bustling through his set like an industrious, inventive soul, ploughing waves of sick blues and garage-rock noise from a plastic catalogue guitar.

'It was the third song when I realised I was in the presence of genius – a cover of Dolly Parton's 'Jolene' played straight, so the heartache poured out raw and pure, scouring all the kitsch from the classic. As Jack White ricocheted into the diesel-huffing hick-hop of 'Hello Operator', I could think of no comparison better than Beck, who'd similarly sifted something new and fresh from ancient dustbowl music.

'But there was none of Beck's sense of irony here, this was something warmer and fleshier, the ruddy-faced boy onstage casually slipping into jaw-dropping but unflashy displays of left-handed guitar virtuosity, dropping impossibly fragile folk ballads into the mix, and courteously introducing his sister Meg (on drums) to the audience.

We were sold on The White Stripes.'

When Stevie and Steve reached London they persuaded the NME live reviews editor to run a photo review of this – so far – largely unknown band.

After DJ John Peel's persistence and the NME live review, months of unnecessary hype (the music spoke for itself) followed.

Peel, who sadly died at the end of October, 2004, was renowned for kick-starting the careers of so many bands in his 40 years as a radio DJ. In addition to early airings of the White Stripes 7" 'Handsprings', he had picked up a copy of *White Blood Cells* from an independent record shop he had visited on a trip to Groningen in the Netherlands. On air he told listeners they were the most exciting band since punk or Hendrix. It was some eulogy – especially from someone of his influence and standing in the industry. And it wasn't long before Britain, too, fell in love with the band.

On July 4th, London's **Evening Standard** newspaper became the first UK publication to run an interview with The White Stripes. Previewing their first ever appearance at Oxford Street's 100 Club at the end of the month, the paper's music pages screamed: 'Big Riffs From Across The Pond: US garage rock is back, and Detroit and New York are where it's at.' Stevie Chick, once again, was at the helm. He wrote:

'Their third album, White Blood Cells, is a work of casual genius that should make superstars of them.'

How right he was.

'It's really difficult for bands in Detroit to get heard,' Jack told Stevie. For this reason, Jack had produced *The Sympathetic Sounds of Detroit*, a compilation album 'capturing 14 of Detroit's finest in their grimy element.

'From The Paybacks' Stones-esque 'Black Girl', to the humorous 'I'm Through With White Girls' by The Dirtbombs, to The Detroit Cobras and their boogie-licious Otis Redding cover, 'Shout Bamalama', it celebrates Detroit's musical heritage as well as sketching its future,' Stevie wrote.

'Black people invented the greatest forms of music: jazz, blues, soul, R'n'B and rock 'n' roll,' **Jack said.**

'There's no escaping that influence… I don't think The White Stripes are MTV material but even if we did achieve that kind of success we wouldn't let it change what we're doing.'

The word had already wound its way round the streets of Britain when the White Stripes made the trip across the pond for their inaugural club tour the following month. In fact, the reception they got in the UK was slightly bigger than Jack and Meg had anticipated.

Hailed as the saviours of rock 'n' roll, even the British tabloids were chasing The White Stripes' story - its gossip columnists standing in line outside Oxford Street's 100 Club, desperate to snag one of the tickets that were now exchanging hands for upwards of £100.

The club's owner said he could have sold the venue out ten times over.

For once though, a band lived up to its hype.

Britain loved them both. Jack with his eccentric phrasing and unpredictable – but harmonically impeccable – guitar riffs; Meg – the pale-faced beauty who could apparently throw down the whisky with the best of them – for all her shyness, oozing Detroit cool.

Stevie Chick reviewed the show for the NME. 'He's the Don of Detroit, the God of garage, the man reclaiming rock 'n' roll from false-hearted cheats and whining, hollow charlatans,' he wrote. 'Let's cut straight to the fucking bone here: tonight, we saw rock 'n' roll born again, stripped back to its barest elements, dipped in dirt and sex and explosive passion, and sent reeling into the future.'

A week later they were at the Boston Arms in Tufnell Park – a rough and ready haunt of local garage rock favourites Holly Golightly, Billy Childish and Liam Watson. That night, as a hack from **The Sun** tried to barter for tickets outside, Kate Moss stood at the back taking in this early UK performance by one of the most exciting bands to grace our shores for years.

The next morning **The Sun** newspaper carried the story – the review taking up the main portion of Dominic Mohan's 'Bizarre' column – the only time the paper had given so much space to a gig in its entire history. Peel booked the band for his Radio 1 programme; the influential **NME** was chasing them for its front cover. Initially The White Stripes refused were wary of interviews.

'In America we heard that in England you can suddenly become big for a couple of months – then everybody forgets about you after that,' Jack said.

'We're trying not to take it too seriously.'

Before they appeared on Peel's show, the veteran DJ took them out for a meal. The three talked about Eddie Cochrane, Gene Vincent and Son House and by the time Jack and Meg played live, they had incorporated songs by Vincent and Cochrane into their set. **Peel was knocked out.**

James Oldham, the **NME**'s then-deputy editor, told **The Guardian** he had seen the band four times in five days. Journalist Simon Price said their colour-coded image 'gave the red/black/white combination an association way cooler than Manchester bloody United'. Cargo's Simon Keeler said the band could be as important as punk in triggering things off. 'There's so much processed music, just manufactured pap for the masses,' he said.

'It's an opiate for the disaffected youth whereas
The White Stripes are a kick up the arse.'

Radio 4's Today programme – usually a bastion of fogeyish, respectable news digest and discussion – had cottoned on too, blasting its listeners with a slice of The White Stripes' garage rock.

Even the **Daily Mail** – that self-appointed mouthpiece of Middle England – said, not a little bit ironically, **'the dynamic Detroit duo have stylishly emphasised that there is a real alternative to corporate rock and manufactured pop.'**

And the siblings/divorcees issue provided the mystery the media needed to keep The White Stripes in the magazines and papers for months to come.

The **Sunday Mirror** ran a
short news story on August 12th
imaginatively headlined 'Trouble 'n' Stripe' in
which its author claimed 'White Stripes, the duo tipped
as the future of rock and roll, are not brother and sister –
but a divorced couple'. The 'revelation' came five months after
both their marriage and divorce certificates had been published in
the **Detroit Free Press**, and after the **NME** had run the story.
But the tabloids it was still hot news. Apparently.

In a feature for **The Independent**, journalist Steve Jelbert claimed he had
picked through the myths to reveal the true White Stripes. Even if Jack and
Meg are really former lovers,' he wrote, 'they look uncannily like siblings... (and
Jack) does seem to have worked as an upholsterer, if that counts for anything.'

One rumour Jelbert did turn up though, still leaves a sweet taste even today.
He claimed that 'hopeful major labels, keen to pick up their (Stripes) back
catalogue, pleaded with NME not to put the band on their front cover
until they could claim some of the action.' But it was too late. By
August the NME had plastered Jack and Meg on its cover,
heralding them as the rebirth of rock 'n' roll.

'Believe the
White Stripe hype,'
Jelbert concluded.

A triumphant Jack and Meg returned to Detroit in November, playing to almost 4,000 fans at a homecoming concert at the city's Institute of Arts. But as well as thousands of new fans desperate to devour every record the White Stripes had made, to hear every 7" they had released, and find out more about this intriguing two-piece by reading every interview they had given, record companies too were desperate for a piece of the action.

Andy Gershon, president of Richard Branson's V2 Records in the States, had heard a copy of 'Hello Operator' off *De Stijl* whilst driving in his car.

'*I thought it was*
absolutely magical,
he recalled.

Following an intense scrum among record company scouts, Jack and Meg struck a two-album North American deal with V2 which let them retain ownership of the recordings through Jack's own little label, Third Man recordings. The contract was reported to have been worth around $1.5m. Buried under the hype was still big money.

In the UK they signed a reported £1m record deal with XL Recordings on Martin Mills's Beggars Banquet label. But neither Andy Gershon – V2's North America head – nor Ian Montone, the White Stripes lawyer/manager would discuss the financial nitty-gritty. Then, they never do.

When *White Blood Cells* was re-issued following the record deals, it sold almost 700,000 copies in the U.S alone.

The press was unanimous. In the world of rock 'n' roll in 2001, only two bands mattered: New York's The Strokes, whose moody punk cool manifested itself in debut singles 'Last Nite' and 'New York City Cops'.

And, eclipsing them in talent, The White Stripes.

By the end of the year Jack and Meg were headlining London's Astoria venue: it was nothing short of incredible. Between those early London shows and their triumphant return to London, the pair watched their debut single 'Hotel Yorba' enter the British top 40 at number 26.

That night, dressed in the obligatory red and white, Jack exchanged glances with Meg as he adjusted his guitar between songs. On 'I'm Finding It Harder To Be A Gentleman', he demonstrated his talents at the electric piano as well and they masterfully re-invented Dolly Parton's 'Jolene'.

'It's the best thing', Jack later told journalist Andrew Perry, 'that communication we've developed on stage. We can read each other's mind, and really make each show different from the last. We started off using a set list in the beginning, but I would just end up ignoring it.'

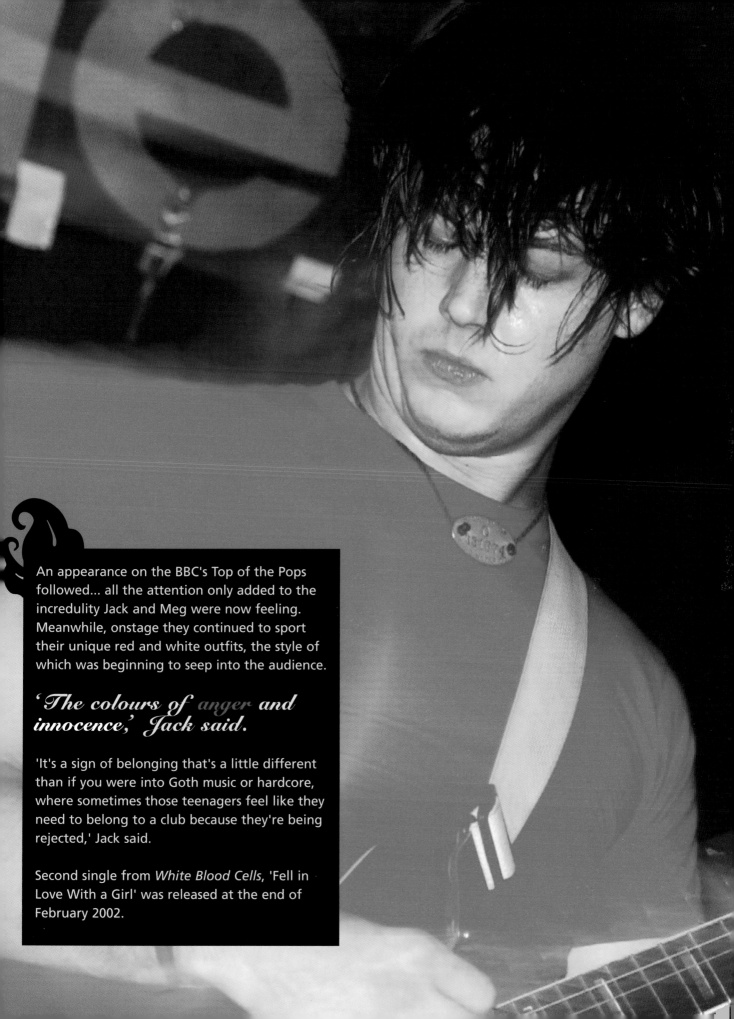

An appearance on the BBC's Top of the Pops followed... all the attention only added to the incredulity Jack and Meg were now feeling. Meanwhile, onstage they continued to sport their unique red and white outfits, the style of which was beginning to seep into the audience.

'The colours of anger and innocence,' Jack said.

'It's a sign of belonging that's a little different than if you were into Goth music or hardcore, where sometimes those teenagers feel like they need to belong to a club because they're being rejected,' Jack said.

Second single from *White Blood Cells*, 'Fell in Love With a Girl' was released at the end of February 2002.

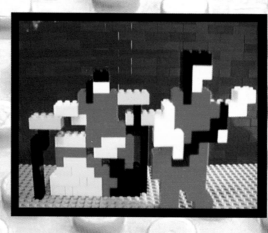

The video for the single was directed by Michel Gondry who had worked with Bjork and Massive Attack and who would later go on to direct Jim Carrey in the 2004 blockbuster *Eternal Sunshine of the Spotless Mind*. For 'Fell in Love', Gondry used children's Lego pieces and stop-motion animation. It begins with Gondry's son, Paul building a Lego countdown, then depicts Jack and Meg – as Lego pieces – playing their instruments and singing.

Each frame was photographed individually with a 16mm Bolex camera. 'The White Stripes music is so basic – drum, guitars and voice,' Gondry said, 'so I thought using three primary colours worked...

I thought the crudeness of Lego would represent them well'.

Meg said Gondry worked in a very mathematical way. 'Everything is worked out to the tiniest little detail. Every second is mapped out but at the same time, there's a total childlike fascination with colour and shapes and sequences.'

By May, The White Stripes had graduated to playing London's huge Shepherds Bush Empire.

The Guardian newspaper noted that they were introduced as 'the best live band in the world', and it then went to explain why: 'Jack White is possessed of a startling wounded howl and a ferocious, attacking guitar technique... [whilst Meg] occasionally plays one-handed, resting the other on her hip like a teacher demanding the culprit make himself known. The duo's interplay is bizarre'.

Two months later the **LA Times** declared:

'There isn't a more thrilling new figure in American rock, and he's a big reason why rock seems to be turning a corner after a drab late '90s.

'The Stripes' music is smart, liberating, witty, teasing and wonderfully sensual, and the two musicians sometimes show a Zeppelin-like explosiveness, complete with Robert Plant-like howl.'

Everyone, it seemed, was trying to deconstruct The White Stripes; describe their sound and get to the bottom of the myth surrounding their relationship.

And so it came as no surprise, perhaps, when it was announced Jack had been offered a bit-part in an upcoming Civil War epic called *Cold Mountain*, directed by Anthony Minghella and starring Nicole Kidman, Jude Law, Natalie Portman and Renee Zellweger. Hollywood too wanted a piece of him.

The same month The White Stripes played two nights, back to back, at Chicago's northside concert venue, Metro.

Teasing the audience with the sing-along 'We're Going to be Friends' and single 'Hotel Yorba', they then launched into 'Jolene', which Jack had attached his distinctive howl. Near the end of the set he let rip into a raw resurrection of Blind Lemon Jefferson's 'Boll Weevil Blues', adding the line

'Jack White, he's lookin' for a home!'

Referring to himself during potted versions of songs was becoming something of a trademark. Jack had got the idea from listening to Blind Willie McTell who would sing 'All these Georgia women won't let Willie McTell rest'. Jack changed the words to 'All these Detroit women won't let Mr. Jack White rest'. It was a joke, Jack said, after he began 'toying with the idea that girls are attracted to cockiness and bad, bad qualities in men.' But what began as a joke had become a trademark little device.

Towards the end of the year The White Stripes had become tabloid fodder – much to Jack and Meg's disgust. They had always felt the music should be the only thing that mattered. But once the UK's red top papers had got wind of this new whirligig from Detroit, the duo were fair game as far as the press was concerned.

That September the **Sunday People** ran a short news story in its entertainment column headed 'Hot People: Jack White'. Far from being a eulogy to Jack's talent or good looks, the article, by reporter Sean O'Brien claimed Jack 'stuck the boot in when a man knocked into him on the dance floor at a small gig in North London.' For good measure, the reporter added sarcastically: 'Nice bloke...'

A month later **The Sun**'s Dominic Mohan ran a story in his popular Bizarre column saying Jack had been hit in a brawl following an argument in a Detroit bar.

It was this sort of unwanted press attention Jack resented and which reinforced his belief that interviews with the band should be selective. As for the relationship between Jack and Meg – as they were concerned, it wasn't anyone's business except their own.

'The one thing the media hates is not being able to dissect someone,' Jack commented,

'so that every little part of their existence can be written as a soundbite in a paragraph.'

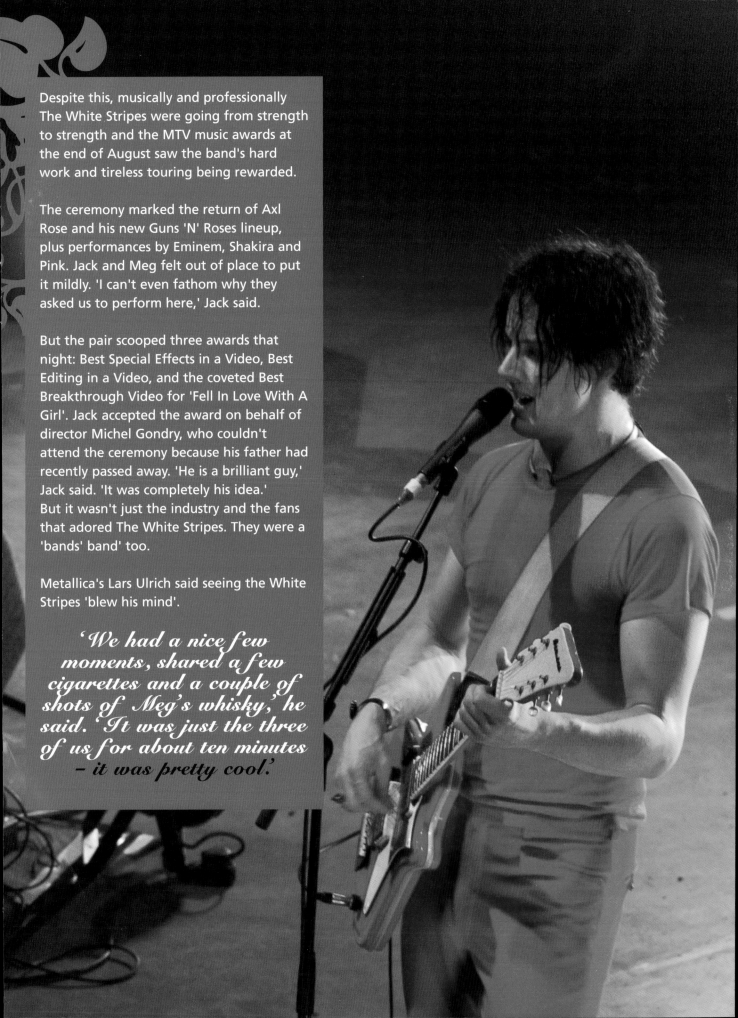

Despite this, musically and professionally The White Stripes were going from strength to strength and the MTV music awards at the end of August saw the band's hard work and tireless touring being rewarded.

The ceremony marked the return of Axl Rose and his new Guns 'N' Roses lineup, plus performances by Eminem, Shakira and Pink. Jack and Meg felt out of place to put it mildly. 'I can't even fathom why they asked us to perform here,' Jack said.

But the pair scooped three awards that night: Best Special Effects in a Video, Best Editing in a Video, and the coveted Best Breakthrough Video for 'Fell In Love With A Girl'. Jack accepted the award on behalf of director Michel Gondry, who couldn't attend the ceremony because his father had recently passed away. 'He is a brilliant guy,' Jack said. 'It was completely his idea.'
But it wasn't just the industry and the fans that adored The White Stripes. They were a 'bands' band' too.

Metallica's Lars Ulrich said seeing the White Stripes 'blew his mind'.

'We had a nice few moments, shared a few cigarettes and a couple of shots of Meg's whisky,' he said. 'It was just the three of us for about ten minutes – it was pretty cool.'

Sonically, The Flaming Lips were quite different from the White Stripes, but both acts were mutual fans. Jack thought the Lips frontman Wayne Coyne was a genius, and Coyne returned the compliment by recording a new song entitled 'Thank You Jack White (For the Fiber-Optic Jesus That You Gave Me)' as a B-side to the Flaming Lips single 'Fight Test'. The song was about the evening that Jack appeared backstage at Coyne's gig in Detroit and gave him a messiah icon.

Jack also helped some of his fellow Detroit bands climb the slippery slope to success. He recorded backing vocals on a track called 'Danger! High Voltage' for his friends Electric Six and watched as the track went straight into the UK Top Five.

He also agreed to produce the new album by Whirlwind Heat and told XL recordings they should sign the band.

Life for The White Stripes seemed like it couldn't get any better, until the following month it was announced the band would be supporting the Rolling Stones on two dates of the geriatric rockers' 40th anniversary tour in October; Jack and Meg would open the show for Mick and co at the Toronto Air Canada Centre and the Columbus Nationwide Arena. Jack was puzzled why but nonetheless flattered.

'That was pretty bizarre,' he would say. 'We tricked people into getting us to that point. I mean, for a two-piece band like us to warm up the Stones?!'

Jack nearly said 'two-bit band'.

Jack, then, flew to Romania where *Cold Mountain* was being shot. The crew had started filming the battle scenes in August but Jack's part was relatively small – he played a minstrel on the run from the dangers of the Civil War, who was married to Ruby Thewes, played by Renée Zellweger.

Singing folk songs to his friends, Jack's character is accompanied not by the primitive thud of Meg's drum kit, but by banjos and fiddles – traditional songs in a get-together that the **NME** described as a 'hillbilly hoedown'. He composed the beautiful folk song 'Never Far Away' for the film, arranged a version of lifelong Georgia resident Fiddlin' John Carson's 'Christmas Time Will Soon Be Over', and sung traditional folk tunes 'Wayfaring Stranger', 'Sittin' on Top of the World', and 'Great High Mountain'.

'The songs in the film, like 'Wayfaring Stranger' and 'Sitting On Top Of The World', are songs I love,' Jack said.

'Sitting On Top Of The World is the first blues song I learned to play. So I just felt this huge calling – that this part was for me. It was a lot of work. I don't think I could ever be a full-time actor though.'

The movie was filmed in the majestic Carpathian mountains of Romania. The cast stayed in Poiana – a ramshackle town about an hour's drive from the mountain, and each morning, at about 6am, the taxis and trucks full of equipment would get stuck behind a herd of cows on the road. It was also incredibly cold when Jack filmed his part as the snows had already arrived at this part of the Balkans.

By the time he left for the U.S, he had become close to one of the film's leads, Renée Zellweger. 'Me being in Cold Mountain was because of how much I loved American and Southern American folk music,' Jack reflected afterwards. 'It wasn't a step in the direction of fame.' He refused to elaborate on stepping out with Rene.

Jack detested the fame game and despised celebrity; for him that concept was empty and meaningless. The fact that The White Stripes' music was – by now – reaching so many people was fantastic, but it was never their goal to expand. 'We didn't have a manager or a lawyer to begin with,' Jack said. 'We were not a signed band. We never sent out demos to a record label to try to get signed.'

Success for Jack and Meg just seemed to happen spontaneously.

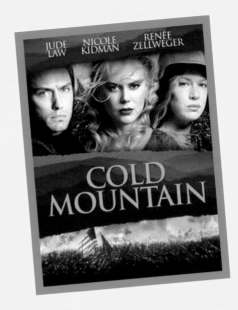

At the end of 2002 it was time to record a new album. Jack and Meg had met Liam Watson who owned Toe Rag studios when they had visited the UK in 2001. Liam also played guitar in garage rock supergroup The Bristols and had produced albums by garage stalwarts Billy Childish and Holly Golightly. His studio in Hackney, east London, was packed with vintage equipment, none of which was dated later than 1963. And when he recorded bands he wore a scientist's white lab coat.

It was all very eccentric – perfect for The White Stripes.

Jack thought recording with vintage equipment would give the album a more 'honest' sound. He felt the tricks you could pull using computers these days – such as artificially correcting an out-of-tune voice – was tantamount to lying.

'I don't consider it a retro idea,' Jack said. 'I just recognised that early equipment like that was never surpassed; those microphones and guitar amplifiers from the '60s were never made better.'

Elephant – the follow-up to *White Blood Cells* and The White Stripes' first new release on V2 and Beggars – hit the record shops in April 2003. It had cost just £5,000 to make and had taken 10 days to record.

Jack's philosophy was clear: 'Every time there's a list of the 100 greatest records of all time, all those albums were recorded in two days. Hardly any of them took a year.'

Elephant contained raw guitar solos, but essentially this was the same stripped-down, back-to-basics songwriting that had made their name.

As is the protocol with new albums, journalists were furnished with advance copies a couple of months ahead of its official release so they could review it or request interviews. Interestingly, however, Jack insisted that only vinyl versions of the LP should go out. 'If the journalists wanting to review it don't own a record player then I don't want them reviewing my album,' he said.

Call it stubbornness – some would say it was the vertigo of success – but Jack's point was crystal clear. The White Stripes weren't about marketing ploys or getting into the pop charts to compete with Christina Aguilera. They were about the music.

And that was it. His philosophy was, if a journalist couldn't play vinyl, he or she wasn't a true music fan.

Even the **Mail on Sunday** cottoned on. 'With no computers to filter or neuter them, these 14 tracks share a powerful sense of space and clarity which lends itself to vinyl,' it wrote, 'providing the snap to go with the crackle.'

Inside the album sleeve the record was dedicated to the 'death of the sweetheart' – harking back to old-fashioned values 'in a disgusting world of opportunistic, lottery ticket holders caring about nothing that is long term, only the cheap thrill' and lamenting the 'devil may care' attitude of people who 'drink, insult, and thank only yourself'.
It was a neat snapshot into the mindset of 'Gentleman' Jack White.

John Peel played a couple of tracks off his copy of the *Elephant* LP on his late night radio show, ahead of its official release. And duly received a letter from the band's lawyers in New York claiming legal action would be taken if he carried on his antics!

The **Los Angeles Times**' critic said 'Listening to Elephant is like playing chess with a tournament pro – an experience so full of unexpected twists and turns that you find yourself trying to guess where he's going, only to marvel at his choices.'

Kitty Empire, reviewing the record in **The Guardian**, said *Elephant* was 'every bit as mammoth as its name implies' and despite a few new tricks – including using multi-tracks –

'Meg still drums like early man; Jack still makes his guitar squeal like a stuck pig.'

It begins with the powerful bass note-driven 'Seven Nation Army' – apparently named after Jack mis-read the 'Salvation Army' on a UK shopfront – and ends with the interestingly-titled 'It's True That We Love One Another', a duet with Holly Golightly in a song which pundits and fans alike would later assume was a reference to the question mark over Jack and Meg's relationship.

But in keeping with the now familiar trait of playing his cards close to his chest, Jack would admit that 'all music and art comes down to love' and that part of the album was about losing someone close, but would go no further. It was just storytelling.

In addition there was the defiant, catchy 'There's No Home for You Here', the languishing, hypnotic blues of 'Ball and Biscuit', and the classic riffs of 'Hypnotize'. There was even room for a track in which Meg took on vocal duties, 'In the Cold Cold Night'.

Gavin Martin writing in the **Daily Mirror** was quick to add his voice of praise to the album, but wrongly claimed Jack and Meg's swift rise to superstardom was down to 'savvy marketing'. It wasn't. In fact, nothing could have been further from the truth. If there's one thing The White Stripes weren't it was a product of some marketing machine or media campaign. The chain of events that led to them being hailed as the future of rock and roll happened purely and simply by word of mouth.

The White Stripes were incredible and they couldn't stay hidden forever. End of story.

By now sales of *White Blood Cells* had reached the one million mark and advance promotional copies of *Elephant* – ahead of its official release – were available on Ebay for £150. Interestingly, the first single 'Seven Nation Army' was only released at Jack's insistence. 'Nobody else wanted to put it out as the single,' he said. 'Everyone wanted "There's no Home For you Here". And I kept saying, 'I really think it should be "Seven Nation Army".'

To coincide with the album's release, The White Stripes headed over to the UK for a tour. In Manchester they seemed invigorated, working their way through the new songs seamlessly and professionally, yet with all the twists, turns and eccentricities that made their name on these shores two years before.

Meg too had a new-found confidence, duetting on 'Hotel Yorba' before bringing the house down with her haunting 'In The Cold, Cold Night'.

The Guardian announced they had broken pop's cardinal rule by 'sounding rawer' the more successful they had become. And succeeding.

One of the covers on this tour was a surprising resurrection of Monster Raving Loony Party founder Screaming Lord Sutch's 'Jack the Ripper'. After learning Jack was a fan, Sutch's son had sent him the coffin his father used as part of his stage show to his house in Detroit.

Then in June, the inevitable happened. The papers got hold of the news that Jack and Renée Zellweger were an item. The **New York Post** broke the story, quoting a 'source' as saying 'They're definitely dating. Renée's really happy about it.'

The couple had so far avoided being photographed together but it was becoming harder and harder. Her star was on the rise after the incredible success of the first Bridget Jones film and she had been briefly engaged to the actor and comedian Jim Carrey in 2000.

Then in mid-July they hit the headlines again after they were involved in a car accident.

Jack had been driving with Renée in Michigan on July 9th – his birthday – when an 80-year-old woman drove into the middle of the street, right in front of their car. There was nothing Jack could do to avoid it and the vehicles collided. Renée was unhurt, but Jack was taken to hospital for treatment to his hand. And doctors said there was no way he would be able to play guitar for the foreseeable future.

The White Stripes had to pull out of their performance at Scotland's T in the Park festival. Pulling out of gigs was a move Jack had maintained he would never make. But this was unavoidable.

Then came the news he was also withdrawing from Ireland's Witness festival due to what The White Stripes website said was a broken finger. At the beginning of August, scheduled performances at the huge Carling festival were axed as well after Jack announced he was to have surgery to repair the broken bone. 'A bone in the index finger of my hand was shattered, making it impossible to play guitar,' he said. 'The break didn't heal properly and surgery had to be performed. Three screws were placed in my finger that will remain in my hand for life. Our shows until the middle of September must all unfortunately be cancelled.'

In a slightly eccentric attempt to prove the break was serious and that the cancellations were unavoidable, Jack decided to post a video of the surgery on the band's website, whitestripes.com.

'I had to re-learn how to play chords with my other fingers,
he would later say,'
but in the end I think it's made me a better player, if not just a sorer one!'

For the band's fans though, it wasn't all bad news. At the end of August, supermodel Kate Moss appeared in what was described as one of the sexiest pop videos ever made. Francis Ford Coppola's daughter Sofia was at the helm of the black and white three minute video of the band's cover of Dusty Springfield's classic 'I Don't Know What to Do with Myself'. Against a plain backdrop, Moss gyrated and posed in a skimpy black bikini before pole dancing for her finale.

As for Jack's relationship with Renée, it wasn't long before the media was heralding its demise. Headlines such as 'Unlucky in love Renee splits from rocker boyfriend' and 'Bridget Jones star in split' travelled round a celebrity-obsessed globe within minutes. All were false of course. At least, they were in October 2003.

Sure enough, by December it was all back on again, according to the press. 'Reunited' shouted the headlines after 'spies' had spotted the couple out and about together. The glare of the spotlight was bordering on the ridiculous. That month Jack appeared onstage at UCLA's Royce Hall in a performance billed as 'The Words and Music of *Cold Mountain*.' The event, designed by Miramax Films to celebrate the release of the film on Christmas Day, featured Jack playing through the songs from the film, plus readings by Jude Law and Nicole Kidman.

But something else happened in December which would once again cause the name 'Jack White' to echo around the global rock grapevine. This time, though, it was for all the wrong reasons.

Ever since Jason Stollsteimer of fellow Detroit rockers the Von Bondies had bad-mouthed Jack in the press, trouble had been brewing.

It just so happened that this time Jack got his own back in full view of the Detroit rock crowd.

The incident happened at an album release party for the band Blanche. Reports of what exactly occurred were vague but Stollsteimer ended up with a black eye and bloody nose. It wasn't the first time an 'incident' like that had happened either. But this time the press got wind of it and Stollsteimer's bruised face was even plastered on the CNN news channel.

As a result, Jack was charged with aggravated assault despite insisting the scuffle happened in self-defence. Wayne County, Michigan prosecutor Mike Duggan told the media that 'far too often celebrities think that the law does not apply to them', but nothing could have been further from the truth. Jack would be the first to acknowledge he is hot-headed but he certainly didn't think he was above the law. Stollsteimer, he had decided, had it coming to him.

If the incident with Stollsteimer had shifted the focus from The White Stripes' music, it wouldn't last for long.

On December 5th the band were nominated for four Grammy awards. *Elephant* was up against Missy Elliot, Evanescence, Justin Timberlake and *Outkast* for Album Of The Year, but it had also been nominated for Best Alternative Album, and 'Seven Nation Army' had been mooted for Best Rock Performance By A Duo and Best Rock Song.

To top off an incredible year, Jack and Meg played a sold-out New Year's Eve show with their friends alt-rockers the Flaming Lips at Chicago's historic Aragon Ballroom. The Aragon, designed to replicate a Spanish palace courtyard, complete with crystal chandeliers, mosaic tiles and terracotta ceilings, was the perfect setting to end 2003. Backstage, Renee was waiting and watching in the wings, while onstage the Flaming Lips' Wayne Coyne, Steven Drozd, and Michael Ivins joined Jack and Meg just before midnight to play 'We're Going to Be Friends' and 'Seven Nation Army'.

When the concert was over and the throng of lucky revellers had disappeared, all that was left was a floor full of black, white and red balloons and an empty stage.

The new year reviews of *Cold Mountain* were favourable across the board. 'A love story on an epic scale,' wrote one reporter. Another said 'With five songs, Jack establishes himself as a well-schooled artist in musical history and a fine performer with his traditional adaptations'. The **NME**, meanwhile, said 'While it's unlikely that he'll pursue anything as historically precise as this for a solo career, *Cold Mountain* proves what most of us have long suspected: when The White Stripes end, White will be far from finished.'

On February 8th 2004 Jack and Meg attended the 46th Grammy Awards ceremony live from the Staples Centre in Los Angeles.

Christina Aguilera, Sting, Sean Paul and the Black Eyed Peas all played live. But nothing could prepare the industry bods gathered there that night for The White Stripes.

Jack and Meg took to the stage in typically understated fashion, both of them dressed – somewhat unusually – in black. They launched into 'Seven Nation Army' but half way through it was like Jack had had a change of heart and immediately slipped into an emotive version of 'Death Letter'. Their unofficial internet fan site Triple Tremelo summed their performance up perfectly:

'It was so left-field for an award show like The Grammys yet it felt so right.'

That night Jack and Meg walked away with two awards: for Best Rock Song and Best Alternative Music Album.

dedication, and one morning, shortly after the awards ceremony, Jack received a letter through the door of his house in Michigan. It was from Loretta Lynn inviting him and Meg to her Tennessee ranch.

'My respect level for her is off the chart,' Jack would later admit. But Lynn rather admired Jack's talents as well, and at that first meeting at her ranch in the Tennessee hills, over dinner of chicken dumplings that she cooked herself, Lynn asked Jack if he would produce her new album, *Van Lear Rose*.

Jack worked on the record in Nashville, Tennessee, and added his own guitar, piano, organ, percussion and backing vocal tracks as Lynn saw fit.

The backing band, which Lynn dubbed 'the Do Whaters', included Dave Feeny, of Detroit's alt-country band Blanche on slide guitar, and they gave an unmistakeable sheen to awesome rockier numbers like the duet between Jack and Lynn 'Portland Oregon', which included the couplet:

'Well Portland Oregon and sloe gin fizz
If that ain't love then tell me what is.'

And title track 'Van Lear Rose' – a beautiful coming of age story in which Lynn recalls her father telling her love stories about her mother.

Lynn told a reporter just ahead of the album's release: 'It's not a gimmick. I've got two more albums in mind, and Jack and I are going to

Strangely, the papers began reporting the ludicrous news that Renee and Jack had not only split up, but that she was now dating Prince Andrew. Fattening up on Krispy Kreme donuts and crisps before reprising her role as Bridget Jones, Renee joked: 'Prince Andrew and I eat them nonstop. We can't get enough.'

In mid-January the White Stripes began a nine-date tour of the UK including two dates at London's Alexandra Palace which saw a total of 14,000 people flock through its entry gates. Flitting energetically from chords to riffs to single notes, Jack rushed up and down the fretboard like some maniac as he dipped and nodded his head, shaking his mane over his sweaty face as Meg kept beat with her Mona Lisa smile, transfixed and anticipating Jack's every move.

Suddenly The White Stripes, unbelievably, had ignited the mainstream; lit a flame in the dominant music culture. They would, of course, never tow any line, but more and more people were 'getting' their music.

And yet Jack was still extremely humble about his band's success. 'You go and see other bands that are really popular,' he said. 'They play exactly how it is on the record, they stop between the songs and say, "Hey, how you guys doing out there" – all this crowd motivation which I'm no good at. I'm genuinely surprised people like us.'

And for Scottish fans who had to deal with the disappointment of the cancellation of Jack and Meg's appearance at T in the Park due to the car accident, they were back.

And the concerts in Scotland were some apology.

When Jack turned up at court in Detroit on March 9th, one newspaper said he looked like an old-school Mafia don. He wore a pinstripe suit and hat to answer charges that he assaulted a fellow rocker in Detroit.

Thankfully, it was all over pretty quickly. Jack admitted he had punched the singer and was ordered to attend anger management classes and pay a £275 fine plus court costs.

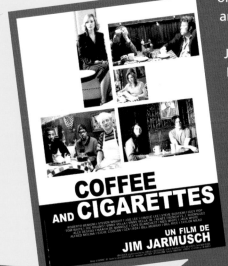

Jack had far more pressing matters. On March 19th he joined his hero Bob Dylan onstage at the Detroit State Theatre to play one of his own compositions: 'Ball And Biscuit', an *Elephant* track.

Although he claimed the movie star life wasn't for him, Jack agreed to a cameo appearance, along with Meg, in Jim Jarmusch's arty flick *Coffee and Cigarettes*.

Originally the plan was to do a video for 'There's No Home For You Here' based on Nikola Tesla, the Croatian-born engineer and scientist who invented the Tesla Coil – a transformer used in radio and television sets. Jack was going to play Tesla, and the video would have depicted the well-documented incident in which Thomas Edison electrocuted an elephant to demonstrate high voltage death that could have occurred with Tesla's invention.

'The budget got a little high,' Meg laughed.

Instead, the pair agreed to film a segment for *Coffee and Cigarettes* in which Jack gives Meg a lecture about Tesla.

However, another movie featuring the pair was never going to see the light of day. *Nobody Knows How To Talk To Children* – a documentary by young filmmaker George Roca – was the subject of a cease-and-desist order from The White Stripes' lawyers. On their website Jack and Meg said they gave Roca permission to film their concert in New York but weren't happy with the finished product and didn't want it shown. However Roca ended up screening the movie at the Seattle International Film Festival regardless after their relationship broke down.

By August the Detroit duo were back in Britain for the long-awaited Reading and Leeds festivals.

And the festival audiences loved The White Stripes.

They were perfect fodder for the music hungry fans as the lazy sun set in the skies over first the south and then the north of England.

The White Stripes would be playing the same stage as new sensations Razorlight, reformed punk legends the New York Dolls and former Smiths singer Morrissey.

Dressed in black, white and red, Jack and Meg exorcised their demons onstage, blending songs into one another and resurrecting potted versions of others.

Renée, as usual, was backstage, adding a touch of class to the proceedings, but a month later, it really was all over. Renée announced she and Jack had split after two years.

'I don't worry about being single because I think you just can't predict when you are going to find that ideal someone,' she told one journalist at the London premiere of her new Bridget Jones film. 'I'm not in a hurry'.

However, Jack quickly installed a replacement, Brit supermodel Karen Elson, then 24. A bit of a rock-chick, Manchester-born Karen had already dated former Smashing Pumpkins guitarist James Iha; flame-haired, heroin-chic thin and punky, she was perfect get-over-Renée material.

Towards the end of the year White Stripes' fans were treated to the official release of a DVD of a concert filmed in Blackpool. **The grainy 16mm film was titled *Under Blackpool Lights* and it was filmed, unusually, using six hand-held Super-8 cameras.** The camera operators had to change reels every three minutes, with no live feedback to the director, and the film aimed to capture the raw emotion of the White Stripes' live performance.

To top off another majestic year, Loretta Lynn's album *Van Lear Rose* was nominated for five Grammys including Best Country Vocal Collaboration with Jack for 'Portland Oregon'. The record had been overlooked at the Country Music Association Awards, so this was a final vindication of all their hard work.

Jack had been a smoker for as long as he could care to remember but by the end of 2004 he had chosen to give up the habit. 'I didn't want to stop but my voice was getting really, really bad,' he explained.

And if that didn't make him cranky, then a lawsuit filed by a former friend would really twist the knife.

Jim Diamond – a larger than life Detroit character who played guitar in the Dirtbombs – had also produced a large number of local garage bands from his home studio, Ghetto Recorders.

The legal action was a copyright suit seeking to establish his rights to co-ownership of the copyright, with Meg and Jack, in various sound recordings made by The White Stripes - including the album *De Stijl* that he claimed to have collaborated on and co-produced, 'providing additional artistic suggestions, supervision and contributions'.

In 2002 the album was licensed to V2 records. At that point it hadn't turned a profit but by the end of 2004, with the success of *White Blood Cells* and *Elephant* to bolster sales, it had. And Diamond felt he was entitled to some of the profits.

Jack and Meg's official line was 'Jim Diamond's case is without merit and his behaviour is rancorous. The White Stripes intend to vigorously and successfully defend this action.'

'Fame and money can only cause them to fall on their own heads in the end, not ours,' Jack told **The Observer**.

'Because if you're not out to hurt anybody, then you won't get hurt in the end.

Meg has never done anything to anybody… how can someone like Jim Diamond sue Meg?'

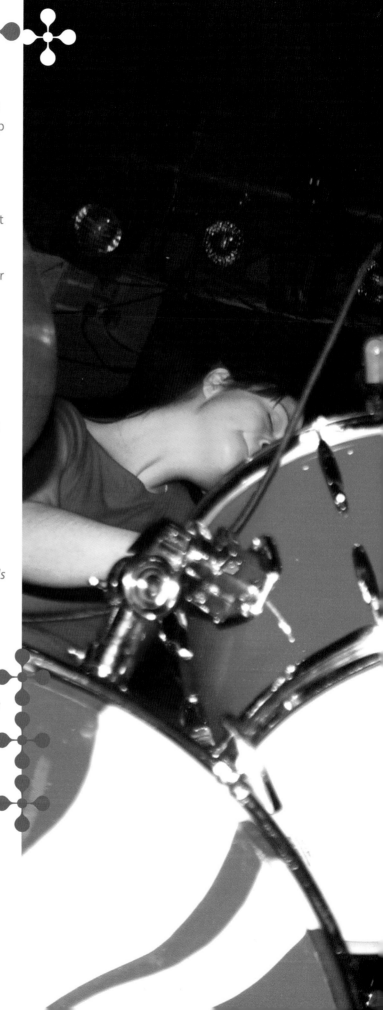

Jack had a habit of championing friends' bands he thought were worthy of attention. Back in 2001 it was the Von Bondies, then in 2002 it was the Whirlwind Heat. But he'd consistently name-dropped Brendan Benson into the mix. 'He's the best songwriter in the world', Jack'd say. And with little fanfare, in 2004 the pair collaborated on an album together.

Of course, with a new White Stripes record in the pipeline – the much-anticipated follow-up to *Elephant* – and Benson's own album due out on V2 records, the release of the dual effort would have to wait. But by the beginning of 2005 the fact that it had been recorded was common knowledge. And some who had heard it had compared it to Nirvana's 1991 epic *Nevermind* which single-handedly changed the course of popular music.

Benson told the **NME** the collaboration sounded like a cross between Deep Purple and Cat Stevens. 'That's a pretty good description,' he said. 'It'll probably come out at the end of the year.'

Meanwhile, White Stripes fans had *Get Behind Me Satan* to contend with.

This time round Jack and Meg had chosen their native Detroit to record 10 songs in 10 days – once again on vintage equipment – and at the end of March the album was undergoing the final stages of mastering.

The record was given a release date of June – just a week before the band were scheduled to headline the Glastonbury Festival.

Initially, all we had was a track listing – an appetite-whetter that in reality just prolonged the agony of waiting. We wanted to get under the skin of intriguing titles like 'Passive Manipulation', 'Forever for Her (Is Over For Me)', and 'As Ugly As I Seem'.

And then there was the cover art: Jack and Meg against a blood-red backdrop. Jack looking vampiric dressed entirely in black and sporting a top hat and wispy moustache; Meg in a period red blouse and wearing tousled hair.

First single 'Blue Orchid' demonstrated a possible new direction – far more rockier than previous singles; more Led Zeppelin than Son House. But the single belied the huge depths the White Stripes' fifth album possessed. For a start the LP was hugely piano-driven. And loud.

But most of all *Get Behind Me Satan was a sprawling, epic masterpiece.*

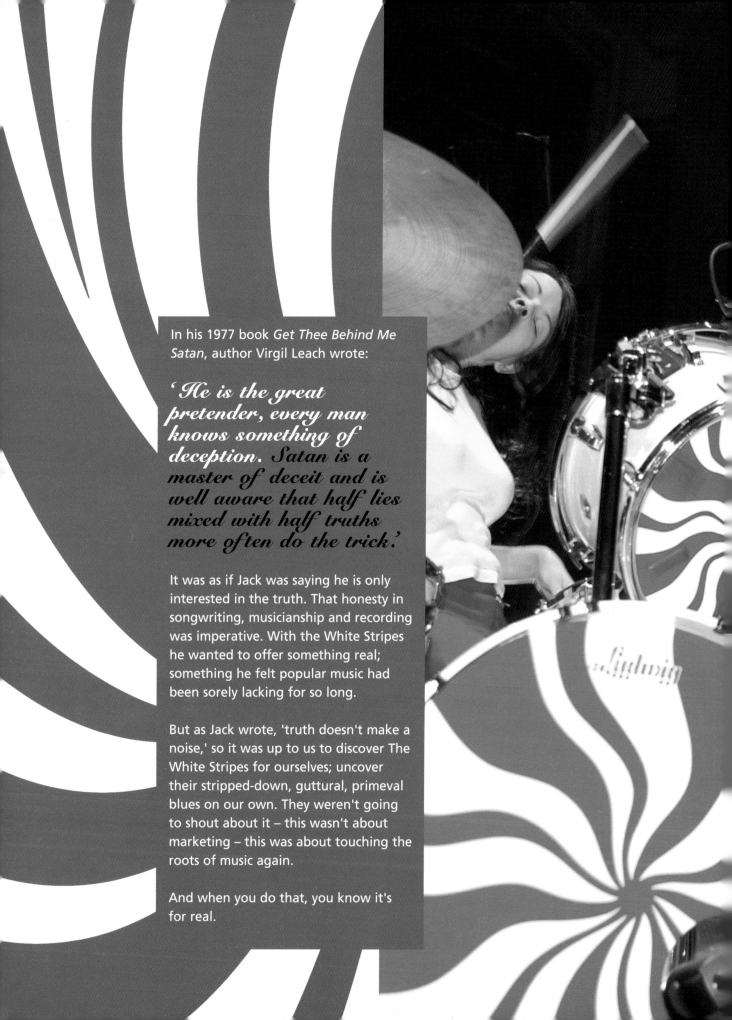

In his 1977 book *Get Thee Behind Me Satan*, author Virgil Leach wrote:

'He is the great pretender, every man knows something of deception. Satan is a master of deceit and is well aware that half lies mixed with half truths more often do the trick.'

It was as if Jack was saying he is only interested in the truth. That honesty in songwriting, musicianship and recording was imperative. With the White Stripes he wanted to offer something real; something he felt popular music had been sorely lacking for so long.

But as Jack wrote, 'truth doesn't make a noise,' so it was up to us to discover The White Stripes for ourselves; uncover their stripped-down, guttural, primeval blues on our own. They weren't going to shout about it – this wasn't about marketing – this was about touching the roots of music again.

And when you do that, you know it's for real.

AND so in the year 2005 it seems The White Stripes may have finally outgrown the grimy, violent city that spawned them – Detroit. *Get Behind Me Satan* appeared to be a sign that it was time to move on. 'I don't yearn for this town any more,' Jack said. 'It's so decrepit.'

He has toyed with the idea of moving away, perhaps even down South. 'That's the real America,' he said. However, a month after Renée Zellweger married, he copycatted her and married his rebound supermodel, Karen Elson. He did it in true White Stripes style: they got hitched on a canoe in the Amazon river with the ceremony being conducted by a Shaman priest. Meg was maid of honour. Where can they go from there?

But wherever The White Stripes go, the fans will follow, hanging on every caustic, perceptive lyric,

*every ineffaceable riff from that old plastic red guitar;
every primitive thud of the drum.*